CLASSICS FOR ALTO SAXOPHONE

CLASSICS

Wise Publications
London / New York / Paris / Sydney / Copenhagen / Madrid

Exclusive Distributors:
Music Sales Limited
8/9 Frith Street, London W1V 5TZ, England.
Music Sales Pty Limited
120 Rothschild Avenue,
Rosebery, NSW 2018, Australia.

This book © Copyright 1993 by
Wise Publications
Order No. AM91090
ISBN 0-7119-3421-5

Music processed by Interactive Sciences Limited, Gloucester
Designed by Hutton Staniford
Compiled by Peter Evans

Music Sales' complete catalogue lists thousands of titles and is free from your local music shop,
or direct from Music Sales Limited. Please send a cheque/postal order for £1.50 for postage to:
Music Sales Limited, Newmarket Road, Bury St. Edmunds, Suffolk IP33 3YB.

Printed in the United Kingdom by
Caligraving Limited, Thetford, Norfolk.

CONTENTS

Air
from The Water Music
Composed by George Frederic Handel (1685–1759)

With movement

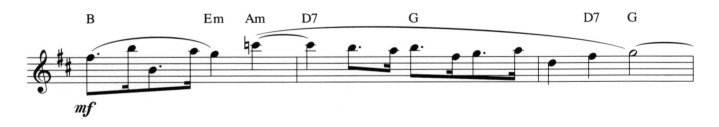

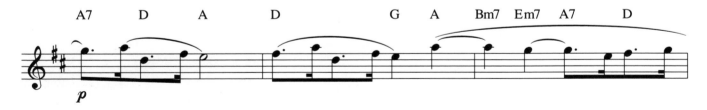

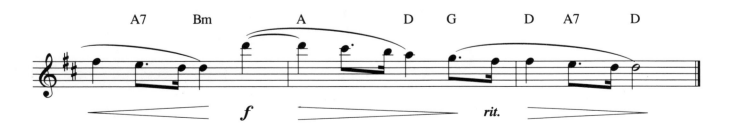

Chanson De Matin

Composed by Edward Elgar (1875–1934)

Autumn
from The Four Seasons
Composed by Antonio Vivaldi (1675–1741)

Berceuse
from Dolly Suite
Composed by George Gabriel Fauré (1845–1924)

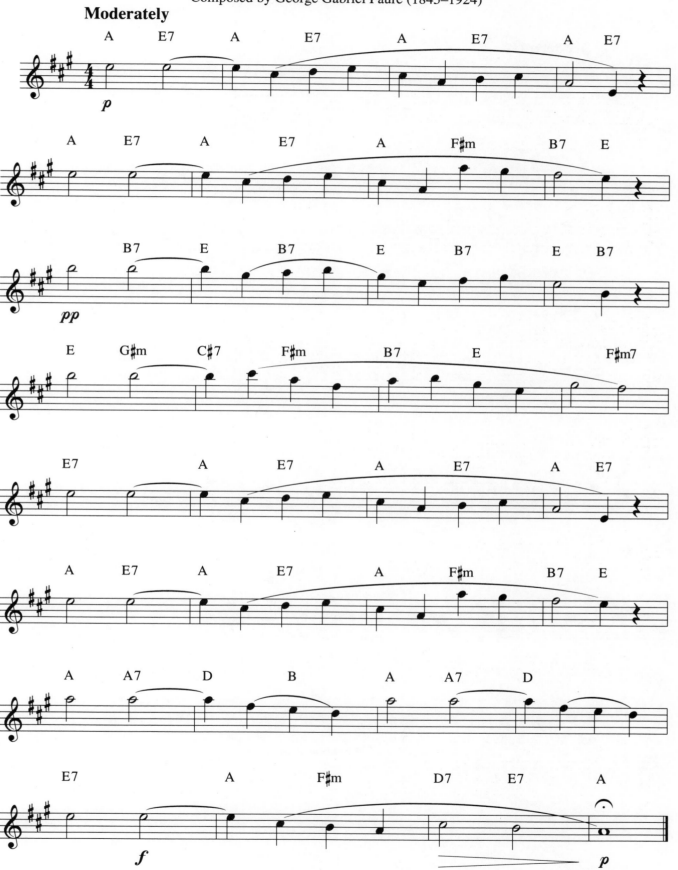

Dance Of The Hours

Composed by Amilcare Ponchielli (1834–1886)

Minuet in G

Composed by Johann Sebastian Bach (1685–1750)

Moderately

Für Elise

Composed by Ludwig van Beethoven (1770–1827)

Song: Longing For Spring

Composed by Wolfgang Amadeus Mozart (1756–1791)

Largo

Composed by George Frederic Handel (1685–1759)

Morning
from Peer Gynt Suite

Composed by Edvard Grieg (1843–1907)

Not too fast

Minuet

Composed by Luigi Boccherini (1743–1805)

Theme from 2nd Movement
Symphony No. 9
(From The New World)

Composed by Antonin Dvorak (1841–1904)

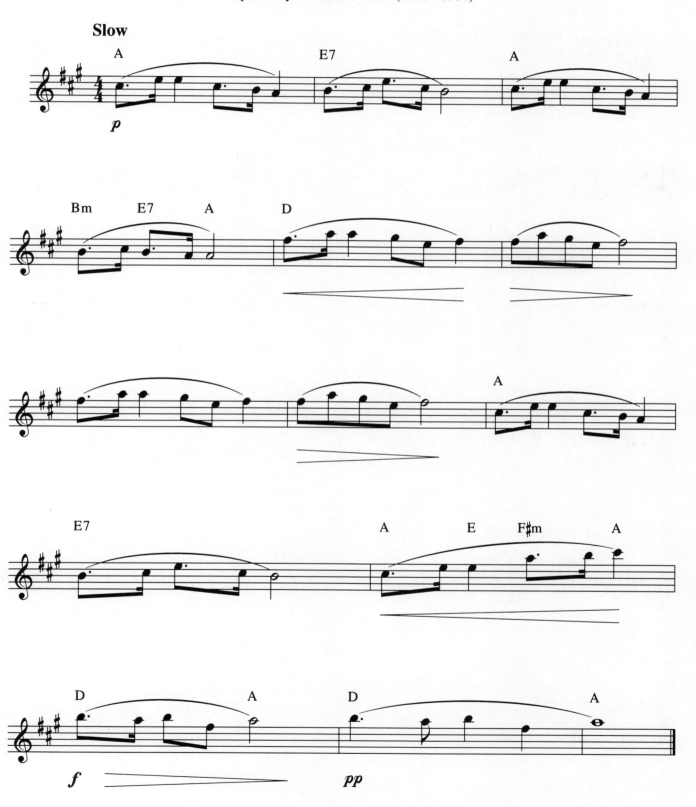

Ode To Joy

Composed by Ludwig van Beethoven (1770–1827)

O, For The Wings Of A Dove

Composed by Felix Mendelssohn (1809–1847)

On Wings Of Song

Composed by Felix Mendelssohn (1809–1847)

Pavane

Composed by Gabriel Fauré (1845–1924)

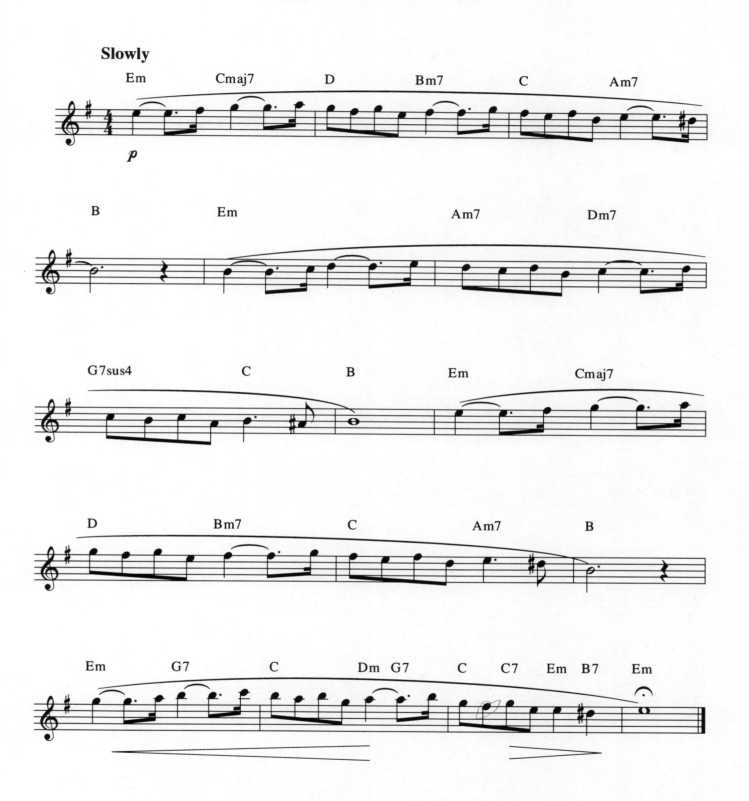

Theme from Romeo And Juliet

Composed by Peter Ilych Tchaikovsky (1840–1893)

The Swan
from Carnival Of Animals
Composed by Camille Saint-Saëns (1835–1926)

The Blue Danube

Composed by Johann Strauss II (1825–1899)

Trumpet Tune

Composed by Henry Purcell (1658–1695)

With movement

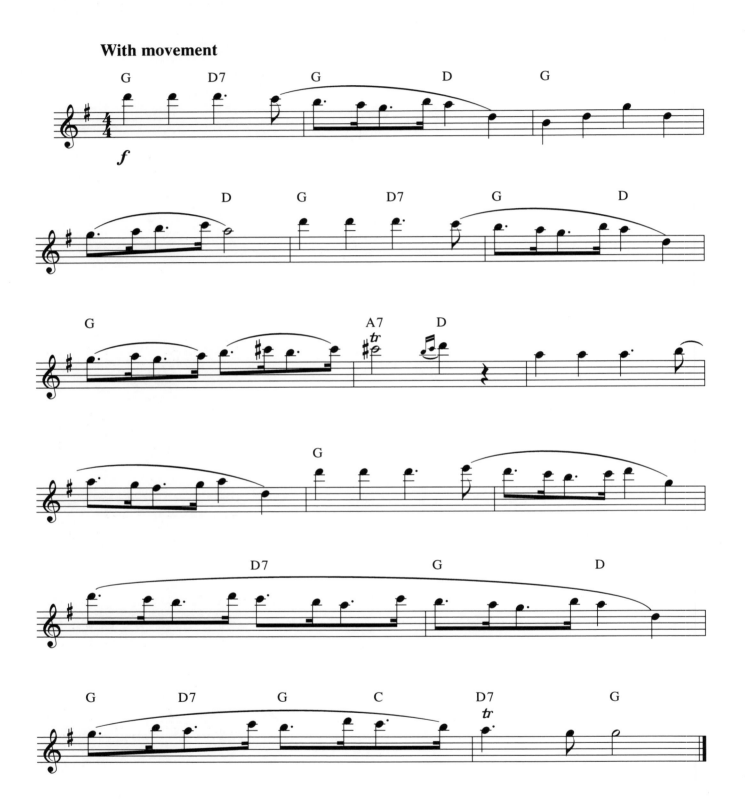

Theme from
Variations On A Theme By Haydn
(St. Anthony Chorale)

Composed by Johannes Brahms (1833–1897)

Moderately

Trumpet Voluntary

Composed by Jeremiah Clarke (1673–1707)

Majestic

Ave Maria

Composed by Franz Schubert (1797–1828)

Panis Angelicus

Composed by César Franck (1822–1890)

Waltz

Composed by Johannes Brahms (1833–1897)

Moderately

Aria from Orfeo

Composed by Christoph Willibald Gluck (1714–1787)